I0673220

Poem of Poems

Dymond Lyfe® Productions

Poem of Poems

Altone P. St. Romaine

Poem of Poems

Published by
Dymond Lyfe® Productions
Email: PoemofPoems@gmail.com

Cover art by Altone P. St. Romaine
Illustrations by Bruce A. Espinosa
Copyright © Dymond Lyfe® Productions

Editing, Book Design and Printing by Falcon Books

San Ramon, California

Special thanks to my editor and friend,
Roberta Tennant, who is, and will always
remain, the sole root of my career.

ISBN 978-0-9815337-0-4

PRINTED IN THE UNITED STATES OF AMERICA

I dedicate the totality of this book to
Trepagnier Etopia St. Romaine,
the eternal queen of the sum of me;
who has not only become the pillar of my hope,
but also the light of my guidance towards completion,
here within my imprisonment.

To you my Nubian star,
I give the poetic gems from the
many deep mines of my heart ...

Acknowledgments

To Abel Leal, Avery Cooke, Luis Villarreal: As
the four winds were destined to unite, we shall
once again after the storm begin the chapter of
that which is written across the tablets of our
hearts...

To my youngest brothers, Elloy Carrillo and
Castro (Tezok):

And each dawn we meet,
Every moon hour we cross
Paths with one another,

We shall always embrace with
Our left gauntlets clutching:
For the sound of true brotherhood,

Sincere warriorship,
Will music our presence
as Dymond Lyfe love for one another...

For the left hand is nearer to our hearts, there
where we hold the gems of our loyalty

And allegiance,
our honesty and devotion to each other.

This shall be forever . . .

Foreword

The poetry of Altone P. St. Romaine has a power and strength which masters the reader...it is lyrical and beautiful, yet also shocking and riveting...the archetypal references resonate with us all...with mythic names of gods, goddesses, kings, queens and distant lands...the agony of imprisonment and the solace of escape through poetry are poignant and pierce the heart. The poems are unexpected, atypical, combining ancient and modern icons...ramses and dean koontz...isis and oprah...rage against the machine and submission to nature. Sensual but chaste, they are anarchic but also deeply moral. The female principle, the essence of woman, is respected and understood, glorified but never dehumanized. The poetic images glitter like gems...rush like crystal clear water...tower like sheer cliffs. This is a stunning masterpiece...an unforgettable experience that shatters the soul and rebuilds it like a mighty temple.

Roberta Tennant
Editor-in-Chief
Falcon Books

INTRODUCTION

I knew I possessed a special ability, a God given gift, when as an antidote to heal my inner pains, comfort my suffering—the constant loneliness of my captivity—I could reach out with my mind, beyond my confinement, and with some preternatural eye, see things that became my refuge. Transmigrating what I could see into words seemed like magic to me at first, and being trapped in a cell for 23 hours a day, anything that could free my mind was enchanting...

I found myself reaching even deeper within, like having your whole arm feeling around in a black hole, desperately searching for a hidden treasure; but in my case, the treasure was to find something new to write about...

Reading became like a savior to me.

Learning about the world fascinated me to the point of worship; I thanked the heavens for each additional book that crossed my path, that carried me further into a new realm of light, of intelligence, far away from the ignorance that had once imprisoned me...

I've never been one to search for an audience to approve of something I've accomplished, and my poetry made me somewhat selfish, to share it. I felt that if I were to allow my work to be seen, the gift would vanish...I actually felt chosen, having such an ability to compose my freedom, my safe harbor from the storms around me. Chosen as in King Arthur, who had been elected to draw Excalibur from the stone...

Years later, after accumulating hundreds of poems and personal quotes, I was enlightened with the purpose for having such sword. Again, as King Arthur, there was a 'Greater Reason' for being the chosen; I held the power to ease the troubles

of others around me, to slay their sadness with words of inspiration, hope...

Today I wonder could there actually exist a spirit, a muse, who enlightens the poet with the magic to see what no one else can see, what no one else can feel...Reading the poets of old has given me such curiosity. How they have metaphorically painted pictures of reality, fantasy, parables to better 'overstand' life and its complexities...

There had been times during the earlier years of my enslavement, when I literally felt as though the suffocating atmosphere of prison life would smother me to death....Lying in the soul breaker, feeling as if God had forsaken the good of me, the part of me that wanted to do right and live just...There in the darkness of my grief, visions of things that had life would pull me away just like that! Something as trivial as visualizing a beautiful flower swaying in a summer breeze could hold me prisoner within my mind for hours at a time. Could this act of captivation be the powers of a muse at work?

I would then return from such escape and write about something that I may have never thought about, or had the knowledge of.

Like my fascination with Egypt. Before I was introduced to the many realms of the Egyptian knowledge, I had a dream about a king who slept in his tomb beneath the ruins of his homeland, mentally witnessing the struggles Africa was engulfed in. My consciousness seemed one with his, for I could feel his eagerness to defend the mother land...

The poem "IMMORTAL DREAMS" was the best of my attempt to remember what I had seen and felt in that particular dream.

I also believe that every poet is a prophet in his day and time. All of the masters, from Shakespeare to Poe, have prophesied about something that directly appealed to someone somewhere with a poetic revelation to their heart's confusion about something or another.

I hope that somewhere concealed in a verse that I've composed is a gem long awaited from a journey someone has traveled high and low to obtain. Even if that gem is discovered by one person, I would be so honored to have given a flame of my gift so another could see what their own heart had shadowed from them...

—ALTONE P. ST. ROMAINE

TABLE OF CONTENTS

A ROSE, THROUGHOUT THE SEASONS

A ROSE, THROUGHOUT THE SEASONS

Be my June,
as the days birth roses before us,
lay with me, beneath the clouds, under
the light blue skies, planted in love as the
summer flowers.
Let's cuddle as swans,
afloat the midnight waters,
looking to the stars above us,
so vanished within each other, not even shall time
pull us
asunder...
With you only do I feel September,
falling as the descending leaves, deeper unto
deeper love, only in thy eyes autumn do I
remember...
You're my October blue weather, my sweet
November,
my tender wind of forever,
soul to soul through the winter cold wrapped tight
in December;
Our hearts knit quilts to bundle us together,
woven in a love beyond measure...
I mean never,
have my seasons changed without treasure,
for everyday your smile promises yet another
child-like adventure, especially in February,
O how I love the way your joy can tickle me
without you even touching me,
hold on to me,
My angelic lover,
and always be my valentine,
not just for 28 days but until the end of time!
March with me,
unto April, and shower me with kisses,

I want you to sit on my lap in May, and
share with me thy wishes, for in your eyes I see
dimensions,
Of flowers,
beautiful colors abloom,
you are my blossom for every moon,
you are my kaleidoscopic rose of June...

AQUA LOVERS

Together is the ocean in which
we must share, through sickness
as in health,
as true soulmates of the aqua,
as twin inseparables from the
same umbilical;
two beautiful whales who exhale
the same graceful air,
who inhale from the same joy
laughter and love...

for even though we grow old so
young and wither away,
when we can no longer hold flippers together
and continue to play, our love shall
not even allow the high tides to
divide us, nor a raging storm to
squeeze between us...
for our final breath shall
escape from the same fate;

our hearts drum as one foreverness,
one reason to even beat...

for if ye asked me to crawl upon
the driest of shores for a beautiful
sea shell, out of thy reach,
to die trying with no sure way
back beside ye,
just the thought of thy pretty
smile if I should return with
thy gift would be worth my death...

my love for you moves as the
greatness of the sea,
long and wide,
untiring,
never ending...

—To the mate of my soul,
Trepagnier Etopia St. Romaine;
for without you, there is no me...

LOVE OF MY DISCOVERY

The art of my heart is as
the science of thy love, the
liberal literature I conceal
in the book of my nature.

Each epistle expressed with
anthems and poems of my pedigree,
that rivers through each chapter
and verse of my totality.

For thy amour is the essence I
use to compose my elations, to
describe such feelings as the
upheavals ye detonate within me,

The expeditions I lose myself
in when taken by thy rapture;
for ye are the mathematician
of my temple,

The equation of my atmosphere,
the brilliant physicist that
brought reasoning to my being...

For beyond you I'd be absent of
geography, barren of the earth's
features, a deserted atom forsaken
by creation...

Deeply buried in nothingness,
I was bloodless before ye discovered
me; a beautiful archeologist, ye revealed
me from an endless somber, then adored me

like some priceless relic, dusted off my
sadness and polished me like a trophy.

To you I'm forever in debt for the
life ye hast given to me,
the sun ye hast enabled me
to see,
the meaning ye hast given me to breathe...

A SLEEPING DANGER

Red as the moon which beckons
a
cloudy day...
like a dark sky for revelations;
black as
the fisted gauntlet of an envious challenge...
hot
as
the
sweaty
palm that unsheathes the sword
for war,
a saber of a passion...that
burns as a gemmed
ember,
that
duels with patience...
sweet vengeance when we taste it...
a bitter
but
quenching
acid...
more sour than malice,
a classical
clamor...a musical rancor,
a venomous
anger;
a sleeping danger...

TO BE KISSED BY A DRAGON

within the concrete clutch
of solitude, I moved as
soft as water,
transformed by emptiness,
I seeped through its fettering
grips...
my ankles and wrists,
became humble to being
wrenched,
my mind elusive to batons of fist...
inflicted tyrantness bestowed
me the secrets of completeness,
to hear the voice of true
righteousness,
to
know
the light of real love, to
feel its
realness, to face the
pain
with calmness, adamant, and
fearless....

to be kissed by the dragon of myths....

THROUGH THE EYES OF WISHES

Through the eyes of wishes,
I ask the stars,
let me have one last kiss
from a winter breeze, be
embraced once more by the arms
of summer;
I beg of the stars,
cover me in a blanket tailored
by spring, so that I may
remember,
In my sleep,
be it my death,
In the fall,
when the leaves of change submerge
me in autumn love,
that nature,
she who breast fed me as
an infant spirit,
cradled me in her soft
crystal arms singing lullabies,
cleansed me with a
smiling,
warming
sun
to ever remember,
her joy and laughter,
for nothing else in this mortal
capsule to me really
matters...

Through the festered eyes of my wishes,
I vaguely see the

flowers of justice,
the birds of freedom;
sometimes I see the sea,
as it waves for me to come,
to hide,
to swim away afar from the
troubles in
life;
I see the multitudes of trees,
the strength of their will to rise,
to stand
before God, arms held high in praise,
reaching for the heavens
matters the storms in
life...

Soul searching,
for the key to
unlock the long
lost
forgotten;
my dreams,
prisoned within a void,
trapped,
embedded,
cast...

unto the lake of emptiness,
the
dead
sea
of
wishes...

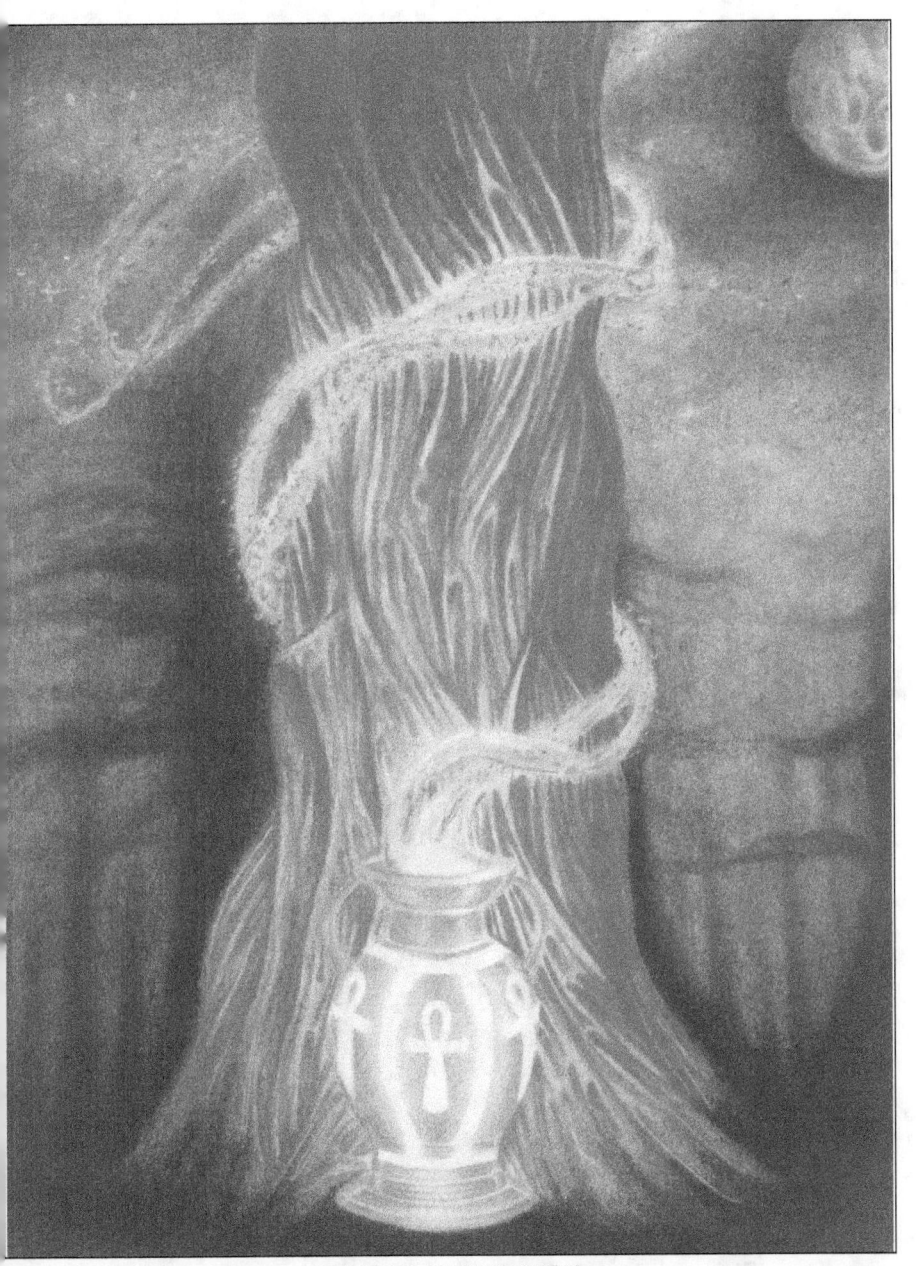

BURY ME TO RISE

BURY ME TO RISE

When the appointed tyme suddenly arrives,
For me to exile the descending of this faulty
Temple, to flee free from its defeat and fall,

I pray to the Gods:

Pour my soul into the finest of soil,
To emerge towards the stars with outstretched
Arms, to ascend strong and tall, able to see

Right into the eyes of a storm.
To kiss the peak of a rocky mountain,
To see afar beyond the norm...

I beg of the Lords,
If I should be blessed to rise a tree,
To feel the many things only their hearts
Can sing, to praise thy heavens from dusk
'Til dawn with no need to cease nor rest;

To listen to the birds set comfortably about
My branches, just chatting, about life as
Feathered creatures, then my Lords, I could
Just imagine!

My ever so green leaves so pleased to dance to
A winter, summer, or autumn breeze, to also ease

Those who shun the heat in need for a cool place
To sleep. To also help the world be able to live
And to breathe;

To speak the language of peace,

Spoken as provision for man as well as for beast.
To be someone equally for everyone...

To watch as the SUN
Each day rises unto the heavens as KING OF
KINGS,
At night bask beneath the voice of his QUEEN, to

Bathe in the coolness of her silver streams; A
Mystery bestowed to trees,
As twilight reveals our sleep with DREAMS...

My Lords,
Please, on the day of my demise, I beg of you,
        BURY ME TO RISE...

SPEAK TO ME

Creator of all,
Alfa, of my beginning,
I have a painful prayer
within my crying soul
I can no longer hold
silent...

Ghosts, my lord...
Ghosts are stalking
my peace with confederate
flags marching behind them
like flaming shadows;

My illuminance grows weaker,
my lord, my ancient scars are
still sore...my wings have yet
to fully heal from those old,
yet modern chains of oppression,

Speak to me...

My only God,
shadow fires crackle like
old whips around me, burning
crosses about me; knights on
pale horses are hunting me....

Lord please speak to me!

strengthen me...
to fight the evil bounding
me, taunting me...
My God,
my only lord,
please speak to me....

IN MY VISION

In my vision....
I see a people fading without a legacy,
arrested, from developing a memory built like
time;

A dream left half pursued...

In my vision I see people self-destructing,
Within a Nubian hatred, waging an endless war
AGAINST THE MAN IN THE MIRROR...

In my vision...
I see a people dying like the last of a chosen,
Yet forgotten breed; vanishing like a fading
mother land...

In my vision I see a people buried,
Like ancient Kings and black Queens,
Leaving a world created by Nubian lords
And magical Gods, for shadowed thieves to
share...
   In my vision.

THE APPLE OF MY DEMISE

Her velvet dress bedazzled me,
like an apple on a forbidden tree,
luring me, tempting me...

Mischief in her eyes was like a glare,
a flicker of mystery; scandals and dares
in the way she braided her hair...

That leering strut was a snare,
compelling me, right into the
manicured talons of her sorcery,

her seduction like a pillory...

Left bound in a spell of lies,
to die; one innocent bite, from
the apple of my demise...

WHEN LIONS CRY

Pridefully wounded...
Embers of thorns of tears of vengeance,
piercing my yearning, that burning of anger;

Surrounded by scavengers...

Hunters of the chosen,
Animals with human eyes like vultures,
Heartless as scandalous ravens;

I gaze towards the heavens...

Be this my final of battles?
To die by the talons of spawns of devils,
To clash with death till my rage hath spilt, my
strength is spent, my struggle to carry on
such war hath ceased....

For I shall neither kneel a captive,
Nor murder my pledge to QUEEN Africa!
For nature hath carved my heart from
the finest of courage,

A rough of the diamond,
Of the bold born a brave,
Spirit unbreakable.

I bellow my poem of war!
Birds shatter from branches,
A rumble of legions of creatures running!

Cackling closing about me...

I peer towards the sun;
To die shedding flames of honor,
To die, still KING of the jungle...

A PHANTOM WITHIN THY TEARS

Lovely are the tunes from the flute she plays,
that whistles to the songs of sadness, a song
of darkness, to charm my flesh, to tease my
pleas of madness....

Her shadow applauds near,
rejoicing to the voice of my tears....

From the valley of the barren,
she comes, to waltz to the melody
of my fears,

To hush my life of all the unfair years...

How she whispers,
with softness,
her sorcery into my ears;

Impels her fingers through my hair,
then a kiss,
then her darkest leer...

PSYCHOLOGICAL WARFARE-MENTICIDE

Silence is screaming from walls with lungs...
delusions are eating my sanity alive...
who are you?
show me your quiet face...
what of my sleep do ye wish to manacle?
once the night blankets the earth, you
come to taunt my hours of rest...show thy
face O cruel and elusive somber, what name
hath evil given you...

Whence does thy voice breathe?
frightened I'm never of spirits,
but ye have a tongue and a mind to speak,
what be ye...

If fear ye come to eat,
then feed quick of mine,
for it pours thick from my pores, then be gone,
for my inquisitiveness hath almost wholly
awakened
to challenge thy reasons...

A CHILD OF THE STARS

A perfect stranger ye were,
seldom seen only as a golden
fish shimmering through murky dreams;

But destiny,
she who lives a slave to kings,
she who breeds the stars of their dreams,

She the keeper of the promise to
birth thee as my queen, to be a masterpiece
within my eyes a gleam, to pose in a gem decked
throne in the kingdom of my soul, en vogue...

You became the heart beat of my
strength, the jewels of my crown,
the moon of my Nile...

Remembrance,
as a wishful prince lying amongst
the flowers of summer, gazing into
the twilight skies thy pretty eyes I'd discovered;

Such a lovely star ye were,
smiling down on me,
so brighter than all the others,
with an absorbing aura,
drawing me farther from the garden,
but deeper unto thy secrets of us as lovers;

I began to speak but could only stutter,
I felt burning within me this silent honor,
to one day serve you as a king, but a slave,
for my heart you would soon have conquered.

You whispered to me,
that I was yours now and forever,
never to be separated, never to be broken apart...

No greater love is there,
than the cocktail of mixed blessings from the
heavens we share, never to be held captive in
despair,
for we own the true elixir of happiness, the potion
to
vanquish sadness, joy to drive away the madness;
all of
the malice, once within our hearts, vanished...

Ye are the melody of nature's beauty,
like a river wind to always soothe me.
Blessed ye are, with the warmthness of a
summer rose, the wings of my every dream;
ye are the magic that makes me a king, the
essence,

OF ALL FINE THINGS...
Dedicated to Danielle Steel

POET'S BLOCK!

Please!
someone release this
lovely prisoner!
To abscond very far from I,
from the barren of my expression!
This eager image,
a burning of feeling I thirst to relinquish...

From the black chamber of
my calloused desperation,
far from the cenacle of one possessed desire...

A struggling beauty so
reluctant,
seeking sure relief from
an inauspicious passion,
deprived of the happiness
of stanzas,
banned from a life of love and free verse...

A shimmering belvedere,
bereft of knowing another,
a consistent author;
tantalized by the beguile of my declaration,
the afreet of my temptation, to cease my days
of composition;

the ballad of my
demise,
her only escape unto freedom...

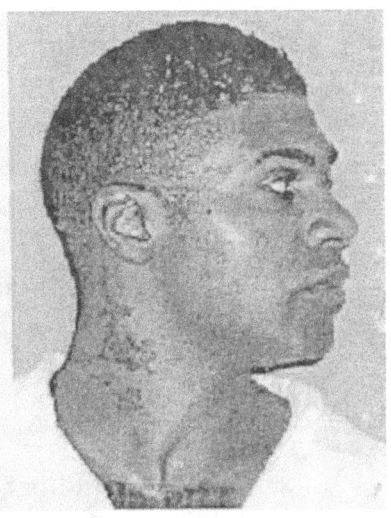

MY SOUL I SHALL KEEP

Still,
as the noose of injustice
slithers around my neck like

an asp,
tightens its grip about my
golden mane, I continue to rage!

To roar aloud as a wounded lion,
and as thunder truly bleeds a
storm,

I rampant,
like fire,
to my final poem

For I die with honor,
even as life struggles
to flee my armor,

bury me a warrior!

a black knight of no more
tears, forgotten pains and
conquered fears

I shall never bow before
defeat, my soul, ye shall
never claim!

Never,
will my last wind be
remembered like a begging plea,

nor shall time sign its
signature across the tears of
a broken spirit

for I invite death!
welcome death like a serpent into
the open palm of my courage, to them

crush death,
with the immortal fist of my soul...

I shall rule with eternity,
sitting kingly on my throne
of victory, crowned,
          INVICTUS...

DEATH WISH INTO THY ARMS

O lodestar of my discovered
happiness, lioness of my devoured
sadness, muse of my poetic genius,

Diamond of my eyne:

should the psalm of fate beckon
thee to a waltz with demise,
thy measured sand seeps through
the hand of tyme's grasp,
I'll beg of the stars
to also close my eyes,
to away
the wind from
my lungs, to join me with
thy kingdom
that hath come,
to chariot me,
underneath thy halo as one...

My immortal rose,
how should I again feel passion
without my myrtle, see rainbows
without
thy
laughter,
why should I live to
only suffer, dare to breathe as if thy
absence no longer matters...

I will not continue on a slave if thou
must leave, shackled by pain,
hunted by the

thought of thy name...

My only love,
if thee were to leave my
arms tonight,
flee from the
garden of my heart, surely
the blossoms ye planted within me
would wither to
ashes,
the sun would vanish!
I would pray to the stars to then
be banished, from this existence,
to never awaken unless
ye are
with me to keep...

The jazz of thy presence,
the lotus of thy Nubian essence,
be
as
the light of my every night
with
stars,
as diamonds splashed against
the
black
velvet
of
my love...

Thy voice nurtures my soul,
as the very music of nature
that gives life from the anka

of her womb,

I
am the
tides
of
your
moon...

MEIN KAMPF*

A double edge diversity,
like an indigo of pearlescent
flames, an evil as beautiful duality...

The rancorous devil of me,
at war with the better angel of June,

twins from a cosmic womb...

A samurai of cacophonies and peace,
simply sharp as an arrogant complexity,

an ever duel to control me...

From the regime of an undecided envy,
I see graves that bury demons once
hung by decisions,

along side a malevolently quiet river;
so
many
facets
within
me...

Running,
aimlessly,
from a mimic that shadows
my easy image...

Exhausted,
to then turn about to find a smoking mirror,
another me;
a reflected shudder...

  *My Struggle in German

Poem of Poems

Tears,
as musical crushed rose petals,
splash atop my enchanted sleep,
a magic shatters...

I rise my eyes...
blink twice to awaken my mortal
mind, remove the webs that hath
gathered in time...

As salty pearlets of loneliness,
thy presence hath seeped through
the darkest of ancient crevice,

As live vines reaching as cries...
Thy whispers, thy silent melodies
of whispers, expose the depths of
thy secrets to me,

Thy unquenched intimacies, revealed
within me, as burning bushes of
purple red roses speaking to me in tongues
of fire,

Thy furious desires...

The rays of thy tears have filled
my lungs with beautiful poems to
sing, thy river dreams

Hath crossed voids into my arms,
as waterfalls of love thou poured
upon me, descending so thoroughly,
far from a new age of time,

Otherworldly,
so vividly,
in through me,

Thy spirit is with me,
about the jewels of my tomb,
within the sphery eyes of my immortal eyes;

O child of destiny,
Goddess of my feathers,
before this moment of resurrection
I nourished a many secrets of thee,
a many moons there in my sleep...

An imposing stranger thou were,
thy stealth steps across the night
skies of my dreams;

I remember thee,
soaring with swans afloat the
vagrant winds of our soon to be,

A many visions of ye,
adorning a marble balcony,
above the chasm of my rest,

Singing of love as a dove in thy
nest to rise me...

O joy speak to me!
through the stars,
between the ether,

For now that I no longer
sleep, amuse me, perform
thy voice for me...
(A WOMAN ANSWERING HIM)

My long awaited warrior king,
the brilliance of thy aura is
as the flowers of my father's garden,

as colors never to be fathomed by
mortals. Thy heart is the chest of
my treasures, gems I've yearned to
gather to cherish forever...

My nubian ramses,
arise from thy sarcophagus,
to prevail as the pyramids of africa!

My lord,
my black pharaoh,
ascend into my arms,

For the gods hath prepared us
an emerald isle, unblemished
white sand strand about,

Amidst the beautiful heavens,
to dance together as spirits,
to swim as naked as all eden...

Come lay thy head between my golden
mountains, wrap thy arms around me,
for before I come forth a mortal,

I wish to hold thy soul a moment...

June, 1906: N. Egypt
Near Cairo

(A breeze of antiquity, a soothing
wind moves in through the tent, to
kiss those beneath who shun the heat)

Sir Akbar: This has got to be the spot, we must
now dig to begin a start.

Sir Stewart: Yes, I agree, I am pleased, this is
most definitely the moment to begin.

Sir Dubois: I hope this site is correct, I must say;
for if it succeeds, we shall surely enter "history"
this bright and sunny day,

Sir James: Can thou just imagine! What if this is
really the great Ramses? The warrior king who
defeated the Hittites–

Sir Stewart: Then that poor dummy in the
museum will prove a scandal of a mummy.

Sir Akbar: Come now, we need summon our
laborers...

September, 1906: Paris, France (rehearsal)

Stephone: Trepagnier, my girl, art thou feeling
well? Thou suddenly look a little ill.

Trepagnier: No, I, ah...

Stephone: Come, come, plaire sit down, ye must
lighten thy feet awhile. Mr. St. Claire, away with
this crowd!

St. Claire: As ye plaire, monsieur. Alright, tout le monde, move auloin!

(lifting from chairs to leave, people clearing the studio of their things)

Stephone: My dear, have we been rehearsing too hard?

Trepagnier: No, I just need to relax a spell, maybe have a bit to eat as well...

Stephone: Thou poor girl, ye do look a little pale, shall I beckon reservations for dejeuner at La'salles?

Trepagnier: Yes, that will be fine, Stephone, and could you fetch my good friend Molly? I'm sure she's out about the garden.

Stephone: O certainly, amour, it will be my pleasure, leave all up to thy eldest brother...

(a moment alone...
utterly confused...
something within...
disturbingly odd..,.)

Molly: Young Trepagnier, what of this rubbish thy brother exaggerates? Why thou look as peaked as the moon on a cloudless night in June.

Trepagnier: Yes, I too assume. But I'm having yet another deep feeling something strange is about to occur...

Molly: Oh my, like the one before?

Trepagnier: Yes, I'm positively sure. And my dreams of late hath conspired with these wild premonitions of unimaginable…

Molly: Now, now, calm down, my girl, let Molly fetch thou something to drink. Dear lord, and myself as well, though I'll have something a little stronger and heavier than tea…

Trepagnier: So, ye don't believe me?

Molly: Of course, of course I do, behead me for being so shrewd, I'm just, well, entirely confused. But I am thy friend, young dreamer. Please, explain to Molly the sum of the matter,

Trepagnier: Well, it started–

(Deshawn rushing into the room)

Deshawn: There ye are! Trepagnier, have ye read the paper?

Trepagnier: No, Deshawn, later–

Deshawn: But punkin, a real live Egyptian exhibition is arriving in London. Here, listen to the caption:

KING RAMESES COMES TO LONDON
"discovered by four prominent archeologists…"

Molly: Deshawn, you idiot! Look, she's fainted…

London

Sir Dubois: Na'im, what dost thy soul feel about the pharaoh's curse, surely we must take heed to his warnings thirst.

Sir Akbar: Yes, that I've pondered the first...

Sir Dubois: And the mysterious pearls, can thou window a logic that will free my sanity? Never has there been such an enigma about the tombs of pharaohs...

Sir Akbar: Now, now, professor Dubois, let's not plunge unto madness, I'm sure the gems hold a symbolic significance.

Sir Dubois: Then please, Na'im, share with me thy secrets; why were pearls spilled about the king's existence?

Sir Akbar: My good friend William, do recall the ancient myth of the Roman lords; pearls as the frozen tears of the gods...*

*It's been said through old Roman and Greek tales that pearls were the frozen tears of the gods and goddesses.

Paris: Midnight. Location: A royal club

TREPAGNIER: (on stage singing)

Song:
Somewhere far,
but so very near,
his voice I constantly hear,

There,
whispering as sea winds deeply into my soul's
ear, stories of promising forevers, of love
as ancient as mighty legends,

Together we'll wish beneath the heavens...

So very near,
yet painfully far I see such a star,
smiling upon me a vow soon to flower,
soon to flourish and vanquish my loneliness...

no more tears to silently drown my heart,
no more endless pacing awaiting my dream,
so soon it shall be, with the chosen dawn,

My ascending sun...

      To be continued...
      The exhibition...

Dedicated to Ann Rice

IF I WERE THY KING

IF I WERE THY KING,
Thy throne would be equal to mine,
I would crown you the Queen of my
admiration,

The Goddess of my only true passion.

I would gift you with the alfa
dream of your childhood fantasies,
a present, wrapped and sealed with the bow
of my heart, served to you, with the mighty hands
of my soul...

IF I WERE THY KING,

I would bow before you as the prince
of thy honor, a slave to catch thy tears,
a brave knight, to always slay your fears.

I would carry you,
each day out unto the nile of sacredness,
and bathe you from head to feet; I would
cleanse ye of thy worries, kiss away thy
pains, then dry you with the warmth of my heart;

Doubt shall never know thy heart,
for I will protect you with the vows
I promise to keep, guard you, with the
sword of my loyalty, the shield of my pride for
you...

IF I WERE THY KING,

I would summon the finest of african
garments, tailored by nubian diamonds,
for you to shine as the light of our royalty,

The radiance, of our new born kingdom.

I would build pyramids in the beauty
of thy name, I would bestow our children with
the stars of night, so that they may never wish
for anything, but own the very powers to create
them...

IF I WERE THY KING...

There,
in the secrets of our bedchamber,
elusive from the innocence of our
glamorous children, I would sing to you,

The 'Song of Songs' as if the author,
I would look you in thy eyes and express
my love for you, playing the harp of my heart for
you,

As I make only real love to you.

For you my love,
would be the melody of my life,
the keeper of the gems of my soul.

IF I WERE THY KING...
I would whisper
my ambitions into thy ear, throughout
the night, I would narrate mighty legends

and beautiful stories of nubian love, as
we dance unto the palace of our sleep, soaring
together deeply within the heavenly realms of our
dreams;

IF I WERE THY KING...

THROUGH THE BARRELS OF A NIGGA

if you could see through
my eyes life would seem
like one bitch after
another
to peer through the
barrels of a brother
fed up with injustice,
beat
up
and
stomped
by
the
system...

all i hear is you saying
that you feel
me,
but if you could truly
feel the pain i've endured,
the scars you'd know
would well deeper
than the diaspora,
deeper than the belly
of slave ships,
louder than the blood spilt
with each crack of the
master's whip,
the necks snapped between
each unyielding noose...

if you could just walk in
my shoes,

the
ones
i've
worn
in
the
cotton
fields,
the ones i've marched and
died for my freedom in...

what if you had to face
your children a broken
spirit,
when all their hope was
relied on your strength
as the family pillar,
to protect your people
wouldn't you commit murder?

when your leaders are gunned down
by hatred, racist!
there's a time to kill
when four little girls
are blown to pieces
by clansmen!

you've looked me right in
the eyes and broken promises,
taught me to turn the other
cheek when slapped by oppression

if you could see what i see.

IN MY DREAM

In my dream I've seen a
wandering queen dancing
sadly beneath a sleepless moon,

an aura of gloom illumed her seeded womb...

her eyes resembled an
onyx pain, a deep shade of
thirsting rain, orbs that prayed
beyond the reach of native gods
who ignored her desperate wails
that shattered the nights and eclipsed her heart...

Forsaken stars trickled down her sable face,
belly infestedly swollen with a bastard child...

foreign bruises adorned her arms
and legs, beaten and
molested to ruins
she weeps
a
psalm
of
heritage...

from her trembling and bleeding lips
she sings a poem of forgiveness,
a song of compassion,

for being so helpless in defending her children...

In my dream,
I felt such psalm thrust hard against

my very soul, ripping and tearing at
my heart for something to hold on....

even through the ages between
I welcomed her my bronze shoulder,
dying to save her from such despair
my hollow arms failed to reach there,

wingless to migrate from my sleep to aid her...

the flames of this vision singed
my ambition, burned my yearning
to comfort this woman.

in my dream...

THE KNIFE ON THE PILLOW

(She selects a delicate number...wipes her swollen
eyes with the back of her trembling hand, pushes
'repeat' on the stereo, so her song never ends.
Picking up the knife she'd removed from his desk,
closing her eyes, to summon the courage...)

My dearest love,

I haven't the strength to carry
on like this, I haven't the will
to longer endure such pain as you've
inflicted me with...

The blood on these sheets is from my
bleeding wrist...my reasons would surely
exceed a list, but know this, your escapades

of unfaithfulness have been like a continuous
stabbing over and over again to the same
unhealing wound...

Today I waited till noon,
there at our favorite café alone,
several times as I waited I requested
our favorite song, 'Endless Love'...

She must be someone very special to
you, Altone, I've wrung my soul trying
to comprehend what could I have done so
wrong, to have my heart trampled and screwed,

shredded and misused...

My eyes are becoming heavy,
i'm suddenly feeling dizzy and light headed.
This must be the start of my ending...

Look to this letter like the very knife
you destroyed me with, the piercing secret that's
been killing me since you began cheating and
deceiving me, my last kiss I'll seal this with, the
words that will haunt you for this...

You were the only man who could
grant me my wish, the king I've
breathed to only grow old and
die with;

the prince who received my virgin
flower, when you held me in your arms
and promised me forever...

How could you become so sour,
to shove me like a defeated pawn
and crown her your lover?

I remember,
the first night I'd discovered,
the silent hint that you didn't
want me any longer,

that it was I you no longer wanted around you...

And today,
today you confirmed my madness,
when I called here earlier and your machine
said you'd left for Paris...

Even though this letter is intended
to stab you, to hurt you for what you've
done to me, I will try my hardest to protect
you,

to watch over you...
your weeping guardian angel,
       your endless love

MY FIRST TRUE LOVE

MY FIRST TRUE LOVE

thou rule upon the throne of my soul,
as the empress of my every expression,
my first beloved friend,
my passionate admiration,
my poetic juliet,

the only heart I've ever shared my secrets with...

my pain,
O love, thou were the
only spirit who could
explain,
for we've twined one
and the same,

and through the low valleys
we've struggled to know the
high hills of praise,
shunned the fame to live in peace,

afar away from the carnal ways...

I'll never neglect my captive days,
when I was captured to die
a prisoner of battle,

ye were my only visitor,

a beautiful psalmstress who brought
melodies to my dungeon, poems
to hush my darkness...

and each time I thought it was
only I and my lonesome, thou
found a way past the guards,

to sneak into my hell,

with thee in love madly I fell.

from here unto eternity my best
to ye I'll give, my every prize
is to thee for the life thou paved
for me.

I truly adore ye,
my every queen,

my sweet darling poetry...

POISON ROSE

the beauty of thy love
has fooled me; I thought
thy thorns would never harm me...

the soft petals
of the hands that
once touched me,
protected me,

have somehow turned into
the hands of IVY, that have
poisoned my feelings for you,

my love for you...

my heart has broken out
with an evil rash, that burns
like hatred,

spreading,
like an eternal hatred...

SPEAK THROUGH ME

O God of healing troubles,
why I hath ye chosen to suffer,
from my mother's cradling arms to roam these
flames,

with cold shackle chains about my broken wings;
drifting farther into deeper pain, breathing in
vain...

Is it I my lord,
to become thy third day,
to be thy prophetic olive burning
upon a sacred mountain, to hold in my
branches thy silent dove weeping of secrets
buried,

forgotten...

O vengeance over my enemies,
staff of my redemption,
kiss me to flee this mortal
cross,
remove the mocking judas
men from either side
of this lynching tree,

those fettered in pity and grief!
Walk alongside of me,
my GOD OF KINGS,
through the valley of
the shadow of
lost battles,
the war fields of my ancestors
unconquerable fears,
and strengthen me,

for I walk alone...

Chasten me in thy will,
my lord, move through
my heart to them of blind hearts,
give me an ear to hear the spirit of thy chosen;
place in my hand one ember of hell, to cast before

the unbelievers,
to ignite a bush of revelations,
to reveal how deep they cover his weakness,
those quiet strings that control the beast...

GOD of my determination,
kiss me the tolerance of thy faithful servants,
to uphold the crown of patience,
to walk across the pits of danger,
to quench my anger...

Kiss me the promise of daniel's vision,
to witness above and beyond the lords of treason,
those thieves of tyrannical dreams, to peer
between the lies of
their schemes...

Kiss me the voice of the seven seas,
to crumble the kingdoms of evil with thy word,
kiss me with thy four winds to sound the
trumpets,

TO DOWN THE WALL OF INJUSTICE!!

As thy elected rejoice unto the heavens,
"THE BEAST HATH FALLEN!"

My only GOD,
speak through me...

BAPTIZED IN PAIN

suffocating darkness overwhelms me...
as i begin to rot here in this
four corner casket made
of concrete
walls...

memories of my
life
before
death
are burning in my head
like eternal pain....

i miss all the things i loved,
once
knew,

all of those memories
have perished in pain...

a fucked up life,
worth of blown years;
an internal fountain filled with mad tears,
unpredictable
fears...

listen...

to the dark rivers of
my sub-conscious demons,
sing a poem of lonelihood...

listen...

to the dark rivers of my heart,
flow with such
noisy,
silent,

pain...

CRUCIFIED EMOTIONS

you have fettered my heart
with sadness, capsuled my
sanity in a nightmare,

murdered my peace with memories...

my temple is void of
laughter,
silent of joy,
empty
of
life,

yearning to collapse...

KING TO KING

If as the eagle I could stare ye
evenly in the eyes, from thy rise
in the east, unto thy eve into the night,

as anxiety wins the great of my plight,
as impatience clashes against the shore of
my fleeting heart; to reach another hour,

To die for every tomorrow,

To resurrect with thy coming aura,
to deliver the message to the ascending
messiah, the golden kernels of truth that

Quest for forever...

Thou art the bronze skin to the burnt face,
the lotus of the never sleeping flower, to
gaze upon the ever blue moon beneath the
identical skies,

To praise the heavens to the rhythm of
a cosmic rhythm, to the likeness of the
rain drum melodies upon the sacred lands...

Scarlet dust I shall return,
to rest there upon the throne of the celestials;

The zeal of my native heart beats as
the great winds of the sea, as softly as
the butterfly kiss I lay upon the clouds a dream...

O as if the falcon I could see!
thy whistle above clouds that music
could never perform...the crest of thy
ambitions,

I shall fall towards the pattern of may,
to bloom the pearl of June, the jewel to
symbol the rose of infinity,

An emerald to solidate the trees about
the wanton grass, gems of a benevolent
nebula...

Talons of destiny apart my chest
that aloof shall rest thy nest,
the great mountain of thy
word;

To join as the twins of the sun,
a third is the eye of our precision,
the fourth dimension we shall soar!

KING TO KING

O FOOLISH HEART OF MINE

O FOOLISH HEART OF MINE

O foolish heart of mine,
Ye who hath become my greatest foe,
Ye who hath become my published ridicule,

My macabre at the edge of the cliff;
My urgence to plunge unto the lake,
Beyond the fire...

O wild and daring dreamer,
Ye who hath murdered my final smile.
For how could you yet again fall prey
to love after all the scars you've known?

To be so oblivious to believe that happiness
Would outlive thy ignorance, that victory
would favor thy attempt to win yet another
race with failure...

For my sudden gladness hath just as sudden
vanished, as the lost island atlantis,
Buried elsewhere deep beneath my
jealous sadness...

O strange and opal creature,
Ye who hath been crowned the clown of
my sorrows are like a silly peasant
begging after every passing chance to

Be handed yet another useless coin,
To accept such scorn with wide open
Arms, ANSWER ME!

Ye selfish and senseless cruel!
How do I claw from you a pain so rapt
from utterance, to portrait a dying
To express my loneliness;

Sculpture an abandoned relief,
Illustrate an agony so pure my vision is blurred...

In my hand stares a diamond eyed dagger,
Very eager to seize thy iron rule of foolishness,
Thy crazy tyranny...

Some good times we've shared,
More bads than laughs, too many
Downs, so many chiseled frowns.

Please forgive me, my mystic friend,
　　　O foolish heart ye are...

LAUREATE OF MY HEART

You're like a divine charm
that plays never ending in
my mind, and until the end
of time is what I see deep
beyond thy smiling eyes;

Something that defies the boundaries
of what's perceived as love.

For every thought of you is
musical beyond my comprehension,
like an amaranth fostered by an
unconditional joy...

For how should one explain
a singing flower with such validity,
and reality, to be so deeply into someone

so immensely,
so intriguing...

You've abled me to be an intrepid
being, a brave matador to face my
foes; the languor I once knew

Hath vanished because of you,
my lamentations hath fled to the
land of nod to escape this king
of no more gloom,

ALL BECAUSE OF YOU...

THY WARRIOR, SENT FROM THE HEAVENS

Like a brave black knight mounted on the stallion
of the winds, when ye beckon for me, I'll rush
rampantly, to answer thee,

Sword unsheathed,
fearless as the sphinx,
honored to die to see you breathe...

I'll be thy eagle when ye are blind to evil,
to soar above you, a warrior king with phoenix
wings, I'd clash head on with the mightiest of
storms
to protect you...

I'll be the faith ye need to move all mountains,
thy staff when ye are weak, thy strength when you

are helpless; I shall cloak ye with my heart, for
the warmth of my devotion, my loyalty shall be
thy
fortress, and at the blink of thy needs, there will
be I, thy nubian genie, with a cure, with a kiss...

Only born,
to keep ye safe from harm,
thy destined warlord, a servant
to you, I vow to always guard.

Completely,
soulfully,
Immensely,
I am thy shield, the sum of my total being.

COLOR ME AS THE SKY

FOLLOW ME NOT,
MY LOVE SINCERELY ANNOUNCED,
FOR I BELONG TO NO MORTAL CAUSE.
AND IF SO, FOLLOW ME CARE-FREE,
MY LOVE HAD WARNED,
UNSOULFULLY, FOR I AM A BEING
THAT WILL VANISH BEFORE I HAVE
ARRIVED; MY EYES ARE AS THE WIND,

EMANCIPATED TO NO LIMIT NOR END...

NO APPLE SHALL EVER CAPTIVATE MY
VISION,
NO ONE BEAUTY SHALL EVER IMPRISON ME.
NO,
NO ONE FASHION WILL EVER CAPTURE ME.

TOUCH ME UNSELFISHLY,
PLEASE,
MY LOVE ALSO EXCLAIMED,
FOR I AM NO SLAVE TO EGOTISM, NOR
MATERIAL TEMPTINGS; NO HEART WILL
EVER HOLD ME HOSTAGE...

YES,
EMBRACE ME ANTI-INTENTIONALLLY,
MY LOVE EXPRESSED,
FOR NO HOME SHALL EVER SHELTER ME.
MY BED IS ONE UNIVERSALLY, THERE
WHERE
I LAY MY HEAD UPON THE VASTNESS OF ALL
CREATION.

FOR I SHALL EVER REMAIN
A CHILD OF THE SKIES...

ZEAL OF THE WARRIOR

I call upon the one true GOD to grant me this
decree, to be placed upon the burning cross of
CHANGE as a sacrificial lion in the people's
name.

To die absent of the fame,
nor be remembered as a symbol of heroism,
but a flame of resistance, not to be recalled
for the blood I've given, but as a brother devoted
to the struggle;

One who has denied himself to become an
element of REVOLUTION,
to lay as a bridge for the righteous to cross,
to carry on the torch...

For there in the fire my spirit shall live on,
there in the midst of those of true merit will be I
to encourage,
to strengthen where strength is needed...

I call upon the LORD of creation to listen to my
prayer,
for ye are responsible for my heart being fearless,
ye
are the author who began this chapter, your hand
who has
composed my determination, to RAGE against the
machine
until death shoves me from this existence;

The only true witness of my heart's intentions...

For I am one of thy gallant braves,
one who wishes to use his sword, rush into war
for the cause,
for is that not why I was born...

I call upon you to listen to my death screaming to
be
freed as a worthy demise; a diamond trapped
behind
these mortal bars, yearning to shine next to thy
other
beautiful stars, those martyrs of the past, for this
is my desire,

Is it not what I am here for...

I call upon you O mighty GOD
of the heavens and earth,
if I am to die a meaningless death,
if I am to exit this life without the scars of
righteous wars,

Without the marred face of a true warrior,
I pray to not awaken in the morning...

AMEN

HONORED TO BE WE

we the proud
wretched
of
oppression,
we who hath worn the
pains
of slavery like a
tarnished
jewelry

we the children of the
river,
we the black blossoms
of
the
cotton fields,

a people challenged to survive, and dared to live...

but we the champions,
we the victors
of
the
earth's
cruelest
race,
we the high mountain climbers,
we
the
adversity conquerors,

WE THE CHOSEN!

WE WHO HATH BEEN COLORED
THE SHADE OF PREVALENCE,
WE WHO HATH LAGGED IN LAST
TO
FINALLY
REACH THE FINISHED!

we the priceless memories of HIS-story,
the hardened gems
of the struggle's
misery,
we the precious diamonds
now
perfected by tribulation,
we who hath bled dearly to be equal with all
humans...

we who hath
erased the lines of separation, the authors
of desegregation, we the change! we the better
tomorrows,

we the people!

A WALK DOWN BITTER LANE

As I walk across
the blood stained
glass
of
my broken
past,
my mind begins to bleed,

like Niagara,
flowing painfully fast...

I feel like Aswan,
400 years of
damned up tears,
my heart plugged with fears;
my
soul
pierced...

As I move on,
on through the grave
yard of fallen legends,
I
hear
a
voice...
distant...
like a shimmering memory,
beckoning to be reckoned;
a
murdered
pride,
bellowing
to
come
back
among
us...

THAT NIGHT OF THE STORM

she clutched them deeply to her
bosom, cradled them violently,
tightly in her radiant arms,

that night of the storm,

to guard them from katrina's harm...

but her winds were
too strong,
beyond the norm,
chaotically harsh...

her children,
those colorful gems of
the mother crescent,
snatched from her arms,
torn away from her bleeding heart...

as the waters rose to swallow
her whole, up above her
shoulders,

not far from her weeping eyes,

the mother crescent looked to the skies with one
last cry...

and through the cacophony of her city doom,
this prayer was sung from the depths of her soul:

ALMIGHTY AND GREAT CREATOR,
I CAN NO LONGER SAVE MY ILLUMINANCE,

FOR THIS STORM HAS BROUGHT ME TO
RUINS...

PLEASE REMEMBER MY CHILDREN,
AFTER THE RAIN,
WIPE THEIR SWOLLEN EYES WITH A
RAINBOW,
PLACE A HALO OF HOPE ABOVE THEIR
HOMES,
DRY THEIR SODDEN HEARTS WITH THY
GRACE,
REPLACE THE PAIN WITH A RAY OF JOY
AND
A SIGN OF BETTER DAYS TO COME...

BURY THE DEAD TO RISE AS BRIGHTER
TOMORROWS,
TO GROW IN THE SOULS OF THE
SURVIVORS AS A REMINDER LIKE A
BEAUTIFUL FLOWER, THAT DEATH BE
NEVER THE END OF THE ROAD, NOR FOR
THE DREAMS OF THOSE NOW DEPARTED
TO BE LEFT UN-TRAVELED:
BY THOSE WE LOVE AND WILL MISS,
BUT SHALL NEVER EVER FORGET...

AMEN

WHERE BE ALL OF THE GODS

where be all of the gods....

what hath happened to all thy colorful
miracles, what hath become of thy
very own creation;

ye who hath condemned mortals
for forsaking their children!
are we now spiritual bastards...

where be the graceful gods...

the immortals who forevered
my spirit, they who hath left
my soul unhealing,

where are ye?

why hath thou turned an empty
care to thy children, hushed
thy ears to the wails of
thy angels...

for we are still here,
alive and breathing, hath ye
forgotten we?

wholly we hath prayed sincerely
to thee for world peace, to cease
this mad destruction upon thy planet,

for only ye could vanquish this....

PLEASE!
why hath ye not protected thy
nubian gems, those burnt face
diamonds from the sacred land
of cush;

they of ethiopia's golden womb.

what hath the original people done
to thee? what cruel hath we committed
to be treated as beast, to be punished
with a man made disease!

where be the gods...

show thy silent face,
for my heart is no different than
the hearts of thy old prophets,
my prayers are as equal as theirs...

please...
weave all thy human colors
back into one people, please...

DEEP NOTHINGNESS

what is it that
i search for,
what awaits at the
end of each road,
to be found at the crossing of madness,
to
possess
that which
is
never
un
der
stood...

each time i feel my
heart is content,
it screams
at
me
for
more...

on starry nights i search afar,
under the vault above
i feel a star
within...at
first glance
i
hear
a
love
un
felt,

my soul giving me the cold shoulder,
rejecting
to
be
found...

something's calling me from an unawareness;
a tempting to fall freely...

i've seen down promises
that had no boundaries,
i've wallowed through
muddy water
crazy to learn
about the dry land...
to
only
be
fooled
by
the
depths of my solitude...

ADMIRATION FROM A DISTANCE

through the telescope of my heart
I've studied you from afar, like a
distant star from an unknown
constellation.

my admiration for you revolves
about my every contemplation,
such fascination is like
nirvana,

anything other than you is non-existent...

at night i lie beneath the
moon and listen,
for the slightest signal
coming from
your direction,
something to assure me,
that this mystic feeling
is some way mutual...

O how i often wonder,
if you could somehow
hear my heart running
wildly behind thee,

trying so dearly to keep
up with thy every move;

would you stop and acknowledge
its devotion to honor you,
or crush it beneath
thy feet,

and carry on as if nothing even happened...

where do i search for the
courage to approach you,
like the lion   desperately
trying to get to OZ,
where do i find such wizard to
grant me the bravery...to cease
being just a foolish dreamer and
spill my guts to thee;

to bow before ye on bended knee
and share the many secrets i keep,
the vision of love i see...

one day,
i shall murder the coward in me,
free my spirit from the bondage
of doubt...one day, my distant lover,
i shall step into thy constellation...

TOMB SLEEP

O how I long to bathe in the blue nile,
walk sandalless through the sahara,
feel the ageless warmth of RA...

smell the jeweled air,
of mother africa.

AM I NOT A KING!
trapped and bound by the chains of HIS-STORY?

a spirit,
from long oblivion,
a pharaoh,
not of this day;

a curse...
for he who disturbs my
sleep,

immortal dreams...

I am
RAMSES THE GREAT,
BEGINNING OF RULE,
ALFA OF TRADITION,
THE EVOLUTION,
OF A LOST HERITAGE:
THE GENESIS, OF A FORGOTTEN LEGEND...

IMMORTAL DREAMS

through the pain of africa...

i vision an evil,
one that roams the land
in silence;
i feel a darkness,
an emptiness,
a shadow,
that has cursed my
beauty,
wounded my genesis...

through the weeping eyes of kemet...

i see a ruins,
a shattered kingdom,
torched by hatred,
trampled,
by the beast of HIS-STORY...

        IN MY REST,
immortal dreams...
i witness a legacy,
one stronger than eternity,
more powerful than
the lords of deception;

i see a kingdom,
furnished by infinity,
a land made like diamonds...

in my sleep...
i flow like the nile,
dancing with auset across the heavens of fertility,

cloaked,
in the royal attire of ethiopia,
the ever soul of humanity...
i am...
tutankhamun,
alpha of a dying royalty,
ruler of a forgotten legend!

resting...

like a phoenix awaiting to rise,
from the ashes of retribution...

WARRIOR KINGZ

harmony is the spirit which
empowers our love as brothers,
warriors,
kings;
we embrace with an overstanding,
speaking in the language
of the heart,
crowned with respect,
at birth a prince;
a day even time must
heed to and remember...

for we are brothers of blood,
as the panther and jaguar,
the phoenix and the
mighty eagle–
african and aztec warriors–
as equals of the hunter,
together we've soared...

the way of the warrior is the staff
of the king, to stand as permanent
as the pyramids;
and the will of the king is as the
will of the sun,
who gives light to the days
by his loyalty to rise...

our hearts beat as one rhythm,
as the very pulse of nature,
we are as equal as the heavens.
your scars are my pain,
your happiness is my savior,

your wars are our wars,
for one and the same be
our enemies,
for together we shall walk across
the heads of our foes unto the
kingdom of Zion...

as our eyes behold the beauty of our people,
as our ears listen to the music of our history,
as change continues to sing from the spilled blood

of our ancestors, we must move with
transcendence,
high above the pit falls of man, and begin that
which
god has gathered us to fulfill,

as the four fathers of C.H.A.O.S.

MYTH OF PROPHECY

My ashes have been scattered,
shattered,
like a diamond exploding into
a billion particles...recreating
the image of a crying constellation...

I,
the soul of the phoenix,
a symbol of breathing eternal,
have arisen,
resurrected,
a many adversities...

for i am we,
the element of misfortune,
the fire,
of injustice...
one,
with the all of my captive,
my native brothers,
immortal kings hidden in concrete tombs...

from the bottomless dungeon
of forgotten secrets, within the heart
of calamity,
lives the fire of change...

a sleeping vengeance...
a dragon,
behind
the
bars
of
prophecy...

LAUGHING STATUE

the lady of 'injustice'
has judged me with a tradition...
laughing behind stone that was constructed
to fool...
she greets her prey with an invisible
blindfold;
holding an off balanced scale that
weighs with a trickery...
judge presiding,
a confederate ghost with a verbal scalpel...
performing mental surgery with a nurse typing
the obvious...
Anig
was the harlot of bitches defending the
secret; Illb carried a brief
case full of conspiracy...

engulfed,
in a storm that has
destroyed my people,
embedded...
in a story at bed time told to satan's children...
trapped,
in a book written by the
god of deception...
as he writes with a pen filled
with third world
blood...

AMERICA FROM THE ABYSS

there i stood upon the sand
of the sea, and clear before me i've
seen a mighty machine,
rising from the abyss,
with seven heads and ten conquered crowns,
and on his crowns ten stolen horns,
and across his forehead a flaming
banner of power...

now the government which i saw
resembled a leopard, swift
as deception,
a symbol of a lost and forgotten evil;
his feet left prints like that of a rampant Greece,
with a lion of a mouth that roared like Rome,

a mythological creature...

there upon this sea i've truly seen,
the dragon giving the beast his throne,
his sacred blood,
and a legion of faithful demons...
and then i witnessed,
one of its serpents,
as if it had been politically
wounded,
and before my very eyes,
his old spirit had been healed...
and then the new world marveled
dazed and followed the United Secrets...

so they worshiped,
bowed facing the west,

who had blessed the machine
with great sovereignty and wealth,
and they prayed wholeheartedly,
unto the resurrected Hades,
who once was,
then defeated,

now again a mighty kingdom...

THROUGH THE EYES OF LOVE

O how greatly the heavens hath blessed
me with thee, for even though i've not
the sight to see,

the vision to fondle the colors that
be, ye hath abled me with eyes relentless,
for through thy heart's eyes my princess,

i can feel the spectrum of true fondness,
insatiable passions of the
beautifully unimaginable,

as sensational rainbows only the blind
could fathom; thy gentleness hath brought
genesis to my existence,

for without ye i'd be lifeless,
fading from emptiness...

for before you came alone the sun
had never shone upon this hollow
home, and never had i known a kiss
beneath a crescent moon could away
my gloom,

never hath i heard such songs as
the poems from thy soul, the goose
flesh ever upon my neck when ye i'm next...

O but love,
in thy voice i sense the shade of
happiness, a radiance so magical
my spirit rejoices!

your laughter blossoms inside me like
flowers, for something precious sings
within me at the music of thy smiling presence.

thy kindness breeds my wonders,
anxious to believe if you could
love me any madder! and if the
heavens should envy the glee ye
bring me, would the angels despise me forever!!!

when i lay me down to sleep, it's as
i'm always conscious, never do my days
with ye end, but only extend,

within my dreams...

DEDICATED TO STEVIE WONDER AND HIS
WIFE,
FOR TRUE LOVE IS THE COLOR OF AN
UNCONDITIONAL DEVOTION TO ONE
ANOTHER...

DYMOND LYFE®

a stone,
pushed from the womb of chaos,
cradled by the hard arms of calamity...
brought up to be
a shimmer of hope within the rough,
an adamant edge to pierce
the injustice,
a gem from oppression,
fashioned by the pressure of
unfairness,
the weight of all the violence;

trampled by adversity...
a substance of the struggle's fires,
we who hold the scars of
man-made wars,
storms,
we who've been
painfully carved the diamond life,
to withstand the earth's constant strife...

we the light,
dully reflected in the marred
faces of the hungry,
those granite faces of poverty;
the young,
the old,
the un-noticed of the ghettos...

for we are a colorless race,
the true shade of an unjust
reality,

suffocating,
equally vanishing...

we are a prism of one another,
common victims of the government's BS!
the system's abuse!
our real enemy be the american machine,
the true beast from the bottom of the sea,
who's laid his demon seed to spawn
this age of disease,
destruction and greed;

his dream of eden for only the elite...

a gem born from C.H.A.O.S.,
a diamond against the machine,
we the true light of change,
to rage against the american beast
until it is deceased, or till death separates
us from our worldly pains...

FOUR WINDS OF WAR

a four legged secret
moves like air, a
silent weapon,
across the
sky...

an angel,
dressed in revelations,
descends from above
heaven...

behold...

an eagle,
equipped with truth,
moves among the chosen...

a light...

soaring like an ancient
warrior,
clashes through a 3-d
darkness like a dragon escaping hades...

as one...

bonding a truth
emerged from fire;
burning like four
winds riding on zanthuses...

WRITTEN IN FLAMES

goddess of the king ramses dynasty,
lotus of my rose garden, keeper of
the kemetic tradition,

queen of my heaven...

give me thy trembling hand, my love,
and doubt not whence i lead ye, my
love, trust in my strength as ye
so believe in the rise of
the sun,

as ye believe in his will to ascend
from his throne, my dove, who guards
the dawns and morrows with equal kisses;

squeeze my hand, my princess,
surge through me the faith ye hath
in me, my love, for we are far from the
reach of fears, my love,

and long before the evils of suffering,
the pains of the soul, we loved as nubian
swans adored by gods, reciting love poems
and angelic psalms of righteous love...

come to me, my bronze swan,
and stall not as i carry ye through the
court yards of forever, my love, for we
shall waltz atop the crown of the moon,
dance between the blankets of true dreams,
my love...

O ye who hath counted the stars with me,
never let go of my protective hand, for
ye are a special stem that blooms my happiness,
bloods my soul, for if ye were to be broken from
my heart, my love,

the madness ye would encounter would burn
eternally; and then i, my joy, the other
half of you, would wander about the
heavenly courts in pain and agony,

wallowing in an undying loneliness...

please, my love,
vow now to believe in me,
i am he who will share thy death with thee,

for if we are not to truly be,
then cursed be god for deceiving our hearts!
AND HERE NOW I BITE MY THUMB TO
ANYONE WHO HATH PROFESSED THAT WE
ARE NO LONGER ONE, BE THEY ABOVE OR
BELOW THE HEAVENS!

to you i compose this poem
with the flames of my heart;
take my hand, my love, before
ye drown in thy own sadness, and be
void of true peace, real happiness.

shun me no longer,
for it is now written...

IF THIS BE THE NIGHT

ready my chariot!
rush to me my royal blue crown,
for if death be upon me this night,

a warrior shall enter forever...

if this be the night,
then bury my heart in the arms of egypt,
alongside the nile of sacred rivers, to
drum a love poem in symphony with the waters
breathing, to feel the beauty of the rhythm of
all things living flow through me...

if this be the night,
then burn my eyes to ashes,
to resurrect a diamond cut falcon,
to soar beside the goddess of the skies an emblem
of africa,
to ever peer upon the burnt face of ethiopia;

if this be the night...
my spirit returns to the womb of AUSET,
then allow me, ye gods, to emerge from the seed
of forever,
to rise from the third orb of ATUM,
to be splashed as brilliance
across the temples and pyramids, to witness the
semblance of infinity,

to kiss the brow of the sphinx with each
ascendance...

if this be the night,

then let THOTH record my contribution to the
stars,
a warrior beheld through the soul of MAAT, a
child of MONT,
O god, if this be the night!
cast my arms into the mediterranean sea,
lay my remains there among the valley of the kings,
to rest next to the immortal undying of the nubian
legacy.

allow me to worship even in death,
the alfa queen of africa,
through my falcon eyes,
this diamond life of eternity.

yes,
let this be the night...

RELUCTANT PRISONER

so high i've climbed to discover
the perfect lover...so long and wide,
i've ventured the angry
waters to find such treasure...

so far and so hidden,
a great wealth my heart had
promised me somewhere existed;
out
there awaiting me,
silently,
so
patiently...

so low i've struggled through
canyons and dark jungles
unbroken,
on through dangerous wilderness,
yet remained hopeful...

for my desire,
the desire i possessed,
had given me the courage
for my quest,
an un-natural strength to never cease
even if it meant to
bring
me
death...

but this gem,
this gift,
was here within me all alone,

held prisoner behind the bars
of my
own doubt, my very own insecurities...
this special treasure was my suppressed
ability, to compose beautiful pictures with poetry;
an unknown passion i've held captive,
a love that will never abandon me,

never ever tire of me...

MORTALMARES

through the windows of pain...
i see dark clouds
above the ghettos
filled with violence and rage,
my people,
grappling day to day
in a pathetic daze;
our future,
bleeding within a man-made cage...

i see my unborn son crying,
his destiny sentenced
to confinement;
like african
development,
arrested and dying in bondage...

through the blood in my eye,
i see change being strangled
by tyranny,
hope trapped by politricks,
minorities held captive by poverty;

fooled by democracy...

HEARTS OF THE DIAMOND

the one with the unblemished heart will be
he who shall defeat the times...those threads
which
weave old fates with new destinies, worthless
deaths

with eternities...
the wheel which spins purpose about change,
and one breath we chance at the last duel with
choice...
the broad way of life,
or the narrow way of the lost...

there will lie endless snares after each path we
cross,
every revolution unto the morrows...
we must keep that one steady pace,
the one rhythm of our hearts to reach true
transformation...

there is no friend,
nor foe,
or brother,
nor mother who can alter the prophecies,
be it the winds of fortune or a reign of
misfortune,
he who is chosen or those foreseen
to falter...
as the seven angels of revelations,
the signs will come...

the purest of hearts will see through the
clearest of vision...the cleansed temple

shall know evil when near it...we must shun the company
of serpents, nor stall in the nets of their presence,

to drift a victim to darkness...

our way is clear,
the way will be our diamond.

our victory was forespoken...

TO BURY, WHAT YOU REAP FROM LOVE

thin is the line between a
glass of love shared
by two,
and a bottle of redrum hidden
in the cellar of one...
a
wine brewed with sour fruits
of
passion,
and once delightful spices,
now spoiled into malice...

there,
in what was once a heart,
but in time has changed,
into something like an open
coffin,

to lay to rest,
all the memories,
all the sweet feelings,

that have fermented into
a
bitter
pain...

THE MAN-CHILD

she kissed him,
passionately,
roughly in
his cradle
like a desperate mother,
embraced him with an early
death like a longing lover...

such a harsh caress he felt,
to never succumb to the
beast,
to ever stand for what he believes...

then came the
red
whispers,
to rage against the machine,
to jam the system,
to plunge unto its mechanism
with the
whole of his
existence...

he was an arch-arrow to our enemy,
a black prince of native emphasis,
a rebel contribution to his mother
revolution;
courage in one hand,
assault rifle in the other,
a soul brother of the king guerrilla,

to die for the people...

to the man-child,
jonathan peter jackson,
the true warrior,
a lion of his own pride,
a noble torch to pass on...

THE MYSTERY OF MYTH

there,
on the dark side of midnight,
behind the blackest of silence
within the night;
there where the rage of angels
roam as birds of prey,
where the naked face of truth
beckons as master of the game...

the bloodline of the chosen,
the bloodline of the fallen,
those who've stained the sands
of time with tears, they who once
turned as the windmills of the gods,

morning, noon and night...

who be this stranger in the mirror,
singing of past memories
of pearly midnights, chanting poems
of safety between the shadows...

but never ask forever to favor you,
for nothing lasts forever when ye
are damned as a mortal,
captive,
within the evil of all evils...

for if tomorrow comes,
the sun will murder our best
kept secret, our best laid plans to
soar,
afar and beyond...

Dedicated to Sidney Sheldon

CROWN ME WITH THY HEART

ye hath blessed me with a peace
i thought could never be found.
touched me,
with a smile that has shattered
my pain...

in thy eyes,
i see a truth ye hath kept
a secret,
a feeling,
ye can
no longer suppress;
an emotion,
someone has scarred...
a wound,
i wish
to
a
day
heal...

thy laughter has gifted me
with the
light
of hope,
a sword,
to slay my vanity,
a promise written
in thy unspoken loyalty...

crown me with thy heart,
for I will uphold it,

as if the kingdom of my soul depended on it....

DRAGON OF SOLITUDE

surrounded by steel
my heart has become
obsidian steel,
colder than steel...

engulfed,
submerged,
in a darkness,
a multi-dimensional conspiracy,

i witness the millennium...

my faith shall guide me
through triple deception,
and pierce 'reality' to
proclaim my throne...

the seventh thunder will
be my song to win; a distant
voice rejoicing, to the last of oppression...

elements of change shall
ride beside me, as crucified
angels sing,

PREDICTED HAS COME, BEHOLD!

like a third day,
our wounds shall heal;

hibernating inside a
secret key,
until the
moon shines her light
of victory...
i rest like a vanishing legacy...

MY LAST BREATH

every night i sit and wonder in silence
where will this road end, all my brothers are dying

while I'm in this lion's den,
i want to holler because the world fucked me,
i should have followed my first mind and did what my
moma instructed,
clutching a prison pillow, searching for some hope
and loving, wondering will these tempting visions
lead to my destruction...

dear lord catch me,
because i'm falling deeper into sin,
demons are playing with my being,
in the hearts of men,
and now i'm leery,
suicidal,
searching through my pain,
with no feelings for hope, love,
or mental healing...
who knows the answer to destiny's voice,
my future unfolds,
praying for something from heaven for my eternal
soul...

everyday i wake up wondering what moma's
doing,
gripping my head losing patience,
all due to mental confusion,
is there solutions for sorrow,
lord will I see tomorrow,

can't trust the wages of my sins,
calling me to follow,
dreaming,
of demons up in hearses on a hellish road,
playing poker, they waging bets,
it's for my lonely soul...

is there a lord up in heaven who can bless me
better,
father please, because i'm on my knees,
and i know you hear me,
at night in bed tossing and turning because i live
the LIE, subconscious laughter drives me crazy
hurting
me inside,
my condition is worse, seems like it's never
better,
i want to fall on my shank still praying to live
forever,
they say thug niggaz don't cry, but tell me why,
my pillow stays submerged in tears, seems like
it's never dry...
O god embrace me, because i'm lonely,
i can't endure this pain,
and plus this pressure got me wondering why
i'm in this maze,
i remember years,
back when i had no doubt or fears,
those were the best of my years but now i daily
shed tears...

with eternal darkness around me
four cornered casket, concrete walls...
strapped in this white man's plan, hearing angels
call

me...visions of freedom, of yesteryears, my life
before death,
now i'm under fire in hell,
holding my last breath...

witness a chamber filled with the heartless,
forgotten ones in camps of concentration,
souls that forsaken,
left hanging,
we on crosses made of oppression,
asking the lord to send a blessing,
remove our burdens,
speak to me, my lord,
my life is in danger,
put your hand on my heart,
put out the flames of my anger,
it's killing me slowly,
i fear no man,
i'll walk your path if you show me,
hold me,
show me the way of the narrow,
because it's hell living in a casket cell,
locked in a cage, dazed,
they're trying to muzzle my rage,
i write in blood on a burning page,
this place is like the darkest age,
like times when we were slaves,
when we were bound in chains,
dying unburied,
with no names on our graves....

with eternal darkness around me...
four corner casket, concrete walls...

strapped in this white man's plan hearing angels
call me....
visions of freedom, of yesteryears, my life before
death,

now i'm under fire in hell,
holding my last breath...

FROM TWILIGHT TO TEARS

as the night absorbs the
last
spill
of
my
tears,
and the moon pours her bright
wine
into
the
empty
well
of my dark cell,
I
close my eyes to become
entrapped
by
her spell...

pull me,
like the tides,
unto thy voice,
into a dream,

for I wish to escape from this
hell,
fly
free from my misery;
embrace me,
my queen,
my only moment of freedom,
sing me to sleep,
so that I may awaken afar from this pain...

safe in the arm of night,
I feel,
when the winds sail in, like angels from
the
sea,

to kiss me,
passionately,
with a breeze, and comfort me,
peacefully
as
I
dream...

from dusk to madness,
twilight to sadness,
only when the day is done,

do my nightmares truly vanish...

LOVE ROULETTE

your love is like being
slapped by thunder....
trying to completely
get next to you feels
as if i'm being held under water...
your love
is like an emotional
scalpel,
conducting an evil surgery
on my wounded heart...

your love...

is a single bullet,
spinning in
a
just
bought
revolver...

ROSES FROM THE HEART

'twas before the violets
were blessed like the sky to
be blue, before the birth of time,

ages before st. valentine,
my soul was conceived for
you.

imagine a lonesome god,
voyaging from galaxy to
galaxy,

anticipating the empress
of his majesty, with a heart
filled with heavenly red roses,

and a box of stars as chocolate
candies for his soon to be lady.

the nights of endless pacing,
anxiously awaiting a call from
destiny, a sign to comfort me,

a vision of love with only thee...

'twas before venus was pregnant
with cupid, before love could
drive you stupid,

i've always celebrated the joy
and happiness you would forever
bring to me....

THE SUM OF MY TOTAL EXISTENCE

all the miles in the world could
never separate you from me,
because you are always in
my heart.

this prison isn't strong enough
to cage the overwhelming love i
hold for you.

my body may be shackled in chains
and hid behind steel bars, but my
heart and mind will always remain
free;

safe in the memories of us together,
deeply in a love that will stand the
test of time...

you have given me a special armor, my queen,
an armor made by the magical hands of your
precious love for me.
it protects me from the evil forces of doubt,
depression, and loneliness; it is also my only
true protection from that vicious and silent
killer, insanity,

who resides here within this ominous dungeon
looking for wounded prey...

you are so alive in me,
that some times i like to
pretend that you are actually
the blood of my life.

in your eyes, my dove,
i see our unborn children,
dancing on a predestined stage under the
bright stars of our future...

when i think of you,
i sense a musical presence,
that fills this empty cage with
a soft, special joy...

one day,
this nightmare shall end,
and become just a fading memory
of a very bad dream, and we'll be together,
forever,

just as our childhood dreams had predicted...

you are,
and will always remain,
the sum of my total existence...

THE BRIGHTEST OF STARS

in the vast universe of business
and entertainment,
i see an afrikan constellation,
of beautiful nubian stars
so bright and educated

dominating the t.v. and radio stations,
running their very own businesses,
yes!
i truly see an african galaxy!
from leaders to glamorous
actors,
from sportsmen/women to judges
and congressmen/women,

rising once again!

black elegance,
the world's most dominant influence,
the most stunning of stars!

i see and admire the ebony stars,
the trends and mottos they've set
for our children to follow,

from oprah to sidney poitier,
from harpo to apollo,
our lovely runway models,
from iman to naomi to tara
and shakara!

the super novas of tennis,
serena and venus,
there's no stopping us now,
we are on the rise,
on wings of black pride!

with or without an oscar we

know who we are, strip us
of our heisman but you can
never cease our magic,

for the juice is in our roots,
you can take our beauty pageant
crown but the memory of our
real beauty will remain unbound,

never to be shackled again,
never to be held down a second round!
our rhythm is in every sound, our soul
can move any crowd!

a chosen people of god's creation,
blessed with the shade of essence,
a nubian radiance,

a gift from the heavens...

i see the brightest constellation,
in my own reflection...

To Oprah,

Through successful black entertainers such as
yourself,
I have found here in my captivity the secret key to
my release, a freedom within me no law nor
confinement will ever again hold imprisoned.
Through the many years of star gazing out unto
the nubian constellation of afrikan entertainers, I
have discovered myself, as bright and as talented
as all the others...

Thank you for providing me with the inspiration
to fly.

A MIGHTY WAVE TO REMEMBER

like the urgent rush of a
prevalent tsunami,
your determination
gushed through life with a
remarkable force,
a power only the vigor of
death could dam,
only a mighty fate could jam,
and yet and still,
thy valiant will
strenuously pushed
and pushed and daringly shoved
and fearlessly fought against
the overwhelming bully of time,
that rude barrier unmovable,

whose hands are inescapable...

you faced the world,
with faith in thy self,
with a greed not for wealth,
but a hunger to provide for others,
a drive to shield and protect the homeless,
in the name of that which is righteous, not

for the fame nor the fortune...

i'll always remember you,
a swaying flame untamed by the rough,
the beautiful bronze clover of my luck,
the hero i will strive to become, whom i will
always love...

to my one and only mentor,
rest in peace...

NO ORDINARY ROSE

born to a rose pushed
from the ghetto's pressure,
a flower from the concrete
of
a
woman's struggle....

i was a hellraiser like my mother,
no father figure because moma was
the only warrior.

my sweet sadie,
my every lady,
to you i dedicate this
poetic expression...

rose mary,
all the times you carried me,
even when i was able to walk,
you still wished to tote me,

on after i left home and
called
my
self
grown, and through each storm,
you not only gave me
your hand
to
hold
on,
i also noticed your foot prints
every time in the sand carrying
me through the same storm...

i felt your battles,
and each scar inflicted
upon your precious petals i felt them;

and even though,
i was a contributer to your worries,
you never once loved me any less
or blamed me...

i must confess,
over the years i've acted selfishly,
frustrated and angry because you never
came to visit, but now i see the bigger picture;

what moma would want to ride to prison
just to see her baby suffer...

if i could turn back the hands
of time i promise every second
i would praise you, and not a moment
would fly by, i wouldn't tell you just
how much i really love...

this distance could never change my feelings,
and the memories when we were happy will
always be my greatest treasure,
to you my heart belongs forever,

rose mary...

THE DOOR BEFORE NOVEMBER

my eyes hath shed a neverending
of thy tears...thy heart,
hath wept the thorns
of my captive
years...

ye have sacrificed thy freedom
to share the dull of my prison,
and i, i hath shackled thee
to the walls of my
wishes...

O but destiny,
how pleasant art thy cruelties,
to mend two hearts to a damaged
splendor, to divide twin
stars between woven spheres...
slit to an abyss as bleeding
wrist, to wallow,
amidst a shallow peace...

be it not for the ardor of our
love, how could we survive the
constant cold storms of separate
worlds;
for me,
to flee the belly of the whale,
for thee,
to flee the shadow of my hell...

awaiting to exile,
each moon after the gnashing
is silent, the madness is quiet,

to enter our garden,.
the secret eden of that season
we fell in love as children...
that door before november,
there, where we store our most
precious of memories...

there,

where we bridge this most awful of distance...

MURDER THE DARKNESS

the Phantoms of my reality
wear The Mask of a dark
secret...

I can smell their thoughts,
and bitterly sense their
intentions...
where do I search for The Key To Midnight,
so I can escape their Whispers
and find a safe Hideway...

the flames of their reasons
are like Cold Fire,
and I'm scared...
The House of Thunder
in my mind creates unwelcomed
Strangers only at Darkfall...
once
The Fun House
is open to them —
The Bad Place that gave birth to my
Night Chills — The Eyes of Darkness
are not from a dream,

but a reflection of my own fears...

as each day crawls into those Twilight Eyes,
my
hopes
become
Shattered...

how do I flee such Strange Highways

in my mind, to be freed from my own
Shadow Fires...

please Mr. Murder!
The Servant of Twilight,
relinquish me from my imagination,
for the Dragon Tears that flood the
rivers of my will are running over;

The Face of Fear you see,
is mine...

The Voice of the Night cuts through me
like a hot verbal scalpel.

woe...
shadow hour is near...

SEIZE THE NIGHT!

Dedicated to Dean Koontz

THROUGH THE EYES OF A DOVE

place thy hands into mine,
look beyond the flames in my eyes,
the scars inflicted by time,
the frozen tears within the black pearls of my
mind;
look into the eyes of a storm now calmed
by beauty,
the violent seas of me now stilled by
beauty...

peer into the windows
of a beast now found by
beauty,
awakened by thy prettiness;
the rainbows in thy eyes have
baptized me in happiness...

through the eyes of a dove,
i see real love,
a beauty as the heavens in love,
i see thee, love,
as a gentle and caring dove,
playing with the once vicious
lions in me,
as an awesome and magical flower,
that has bedazzled all the beast
of me, re-natured the flaws of me...

i see thee as a dream,
my oasis of eternal glee,
the only true love I need...

nomore,
are my eyes as ravens,
my spirit a tempest,

shackled in torments...
nomore,
screeching poems of hostility,
violence from the once belligerent
pride of my lions;
you've ceased the cries of my chiseled
loneliness, saved me,

from the serpents of my savaged garden...

TO DIE BEFORE DEATH

already,
i hear the drums,
i vision a dance,

a tribe,
performing a ritual,
one declared when a warrior,

he who has died for the people,
the struggle
has separated

from the flesh,
ascended unto the heavens,
to be crowned by eternity,

forever a warrior...

already...
i feel the flames,
those that will encircle me,

when my heart beats nomore,
hurts nomore...

TO DIE FOR THE PEOPLE

my armor is one made by
struggle,
tested by struggle,
worn by brothers before me,
who've died in the struggle;
a righteous gift,
to those born in the struggle...

my life is one calculated
by vengeance,
an end written in rebellious
blood;
a
day marked by retribution...

my love for the people is a love
that shall suffocate the beast,
jam the machine,
one day help bring down the machine...

my existence was chosen
as a tool for change,
an instrument for
deliverance;

a weapon of war...

thou shall walk in the name of change,
teach in the name of change, aid in the
name of revolution;

thou shall die,
in the name of the people...

dedicated to george jackson: rest in peace there in
thy warrior's sleep...

ANYTHING FOR THY INNOCENCE

MY EBONY PRECIOUS,
MY BABY PRINCESS,
MY GOLDEN CLOVER,
DIAMOND OF MY HEART:

thy infant beauty is as the color of love to me,
an unblemished and innocent glamour that
ribbons
my spirit with glee...

such an overwhelming awesome ye are, my dove,
if I could die for thy many pains to come,
to cover thy eyes from the cruel of
this evil world;
to protect thy heart from the hurt ye shall surely
inherit, then, dear love, I would rush to the cross
un-hesitant,
as a sacrifice for thy tears,
be proudly crowned with thorns to prevent thy
sadness
and fears;
give my blood to cleanse thy dreams of
nightmares in
your wondering years...

If I had my way,
I would seize thy natural growth,
I would cease ye from ever becoming an adult;
If I had the power, my nubian flower,

thy feet would never know the sands of time,
for I would carry ye beyond the
end of all times,

until the sun no longer shines,
until all the stars hath fallen from the skies;
until my arms hath stiffened to granite,
until I become an old and crumbling effigy;

remembered as thy over protective daddy...

TO MY UNBORN SUN

to my unborn sun,
whom I may never see
dawn from the darkness,
to thee I leave my legacy of dignity...

the morrows for thy father
are far from promised,
a prisoner of war held captive
from the final battles...

for C.H.A.O.S. hath claimed
lords in every country,
every nation hath
turned against another;

brothers betraying each other...

the times hath washed upon
the lands, prophetic tides
of signs foreseen to come...

all around I see flames
licking at the dark smoked
skies above, in every
direction,
death rides the vagrant
winds of CHANGE...

seven months pregnant was
thy mother the last I held
her, the last red dawn I
felt thy desperate
movement in the womb against
my anxious palm...

should I not live to see another
new moon, to know another lemon
kiss of the sun and morning
dew,

know that thy father died
a warrior, uncounted amongst
the broken men,
who've begged to live a slave,
to die without their freedom!
who've fallen a disgrace to the
last of our vanishing people!

Remember, my prince,
that thy freedom be not a privilege,
but a birth right to all things breathing...
for ye are a descendant of kings,

an offspring of a majestic people of royalty!

carry on our legacy,
our treasured dignity,
for our pride wells deeper
than the many seas of oppression
that hath tried to drown us, for we
hath come through storms dragging heavy

chains about our necks,
dangled from trees still
unbroken in death!

Never, my sun,
never let another man misguide you,
never let the unwise man sell you
tales that ye are of a savage people!

I say but never turn bitter
or become a racist, for that
is not in us;

we are a pure and righteous
people, whose love is for
all of God's creation...

pray soulfully for thy enemies,
but never, never before them turn
the other cheek...

the guards hath come, my sun,
heed my spirit when
the time is
chosen...

From Altone P. St. Romaine's next Book, Dear Storm—If I Live to See the Morrow: A Prison Diary

The following excerpts are taken from the Author's personal journal kept during almost two decades in an American prison. It will be published as a full-length book by Dymond Lyfe (T) Productions.

Dear Storm...

Everything I explain about my childhood is from what I remember only. I and the sum total of my family do not communicate so I have no help detailing certain events from my past.

Though the devil of time has shoved me far away from my people, separated me from those I truly love, I will never alter, nor fabricate, the existing unity we once shared under the same roof.

The Nubian queen who raised me was a tremendously strong/self-determined mother who fought and struggled against the forces of poverty. Never once did she search vainly for a man to support her or the seven kids she'd raised alone since their conception.

***

The house I grew up in seemed real big to me as a child. Although it was only a one-story wooden home, it had a big front and back yard... About thirty yards to the right of our house was a railroad track that could be seen from our bedroom window that gave us a perfect view of the trains when they passed through the night. Me and my brothers Reggie and Kevin shared the same room which was cool with us because we had all feared the dark so we worshiped each other's company.

***

The...major episodes I remember from those days are the fights my parents had. They were predictable and routine. My father was a demonic alcoholic, a failure, who was extremely ignorant and uneducated with a suffocating presence that seemed to hang in the air even when he wasn't around. The beatings he punished my mother with were more like energon cubes that she collected—like the ones on that cartoon The Transformers, which were used to store up power.

With each additional fight they had momma became stronger and stronger; defeating my father with the same strength he bestowed upon her; striking back with a boldness that on several occasions drove his ass right back into whatever hole he'd crawled out of.

I can remember a time when my brother Reggie and I had been sitting under a big tree in our front yard on a blanket, enjoying each other's company alone with the summer breeze, when my daddy pulled up in front of the house in this black car. Before he could turn the engine off, momma came racing from the house screaming for us to get inside and lock the doors. His visits were always uncalculated because he stayed in Louisiana so we never knew when he was going to just pop up. Sensing danger, Reggie and I immediately began to cry. It was obvious to us, even at such a young age, what was about to transpire. After we had all the doors locked and the opened windows shut, momma came rushing from her room holding a little nickel-plated gun and stood erect before the living room entrance, peering through the peephole.

Most of the time, our neighbors would summon the cops in fear that my daddy would one day kill my mother. He stood right at six four or six five, damn near three hundred pounds, solid. My mother was a very small woman in those days, about five three weighing close to a hundred and twenty five pounds, if that.

We could hear my father cussing and bellowing even before he reached the door and he commenced banging. As soon as he approached our front door, he didn't hesitate with his intentions; he begun kicking and throwing all of his weight furiously into the door, which sounded like a battle ram clashing thunderously against our home. Before he could bust the door down, momma yelled, "If you open this door, I'll blow yo god damn brains out!!" She sounded like a totally different person when she declared her warning which scared the shit out of us even more. Her voice had been seriously deep and evil. We weren't the only ones who'd noticed the monster speaking through momma because the banging and shit had stopped. My father quickly got back into his car and got the fuck away from our home.

When momma turned away from the door, satisfied that my father had backed down, and faced her frightened children, all it took was her smile to reassure us that everything was going to be all right.

I used to think that my daddy was really insane. No matter how often momma would threaten to take his life, his stupid ass would keep coming back to call her bluff. I can safely say that each time he came back some supernatural being was protecting him.

The same day my mother threatened to blow my father's head off, was the same night she almost succeeded. My brothers and sisters and I had been bunched up in front of the television (where we spent the majority of our youth) watching the Incredible Hulk when Reggie whispered into my ear, "I think I hear something trying to get through the back door." I began hearing someone turning the back door-knob left, then right, left, then right, then a pause. My mother had been in her bedroom asleep, but was up and alert when we all approached the side of her bed and fear-fully explained what was going on.

Momma told me, of all children, to go back into the living room and turn the TV off. Although it was only like fifteen feet away from her room, I told Reggie to come with me. When we returned, momma was impatiently pushing the dial tone button. "The son of a bitch done cut the line," she explained angrily. As she slammed the phone down with her left hand, she reached under the pillow with her right for her weapon. I remember witnessing my brothers' and sisters' frightened expressions when momma started loading her gun.

Daddy had stopped trying to use the element of surprise and began thrashing upon the back door. Momma must have been expecting my father to pull some type of stunt, because earlier that day we had helped her board up the back door, and nailed the majority of the windows shut. The banging had ceased. Since daddy knew we couldn't call the cops before he entered the house, he madly broke out the window to our bedroom and was strenuously trying to crawl through it when we rushed to the back and found him hanging half way in the house.

Momma often told us never to cry when she was battling my father because it would strengthen her to know that we were 100% unafraid. I inherited my mother's prideful ways. Anyone in life declaring to challenge my courage, whether it be a petty or major confrontation, no matter the degree, I have always defended my dignity. This is how my mother raised me. This is how I've forever known my Nubian queen to stand firm through the storms of oppression, head held high and unbowed.

She walked right up to my father as he struggled to get through the window, and pointed her gun to the back of his head and pulled the trigger, but the damned thing had jammed!

She kept the gun to his head, hypnotized by rage, and continued to squeeze the trigger but nothing happened. My father looked up at her and displayed an evil laugh that ran ice cold chills through my shivering body. Pissed off that the damn gun didn't work, momma threw it at my father's head and ran back to her bedroom. This time, she grabbed a gun she had no doubt would perform, my grandfather's double-barrel shotgun. But it was too late. The only reason she didn't blast his ass on sight was because we had been in the way; daddy took advantage of this. He knew my mother wouldn't fire as long as we were in the way. The next thing I knew, Charlotte was screaming hysterically at my father to leave our mother alone. I ran up to him and started pushing him as hard as I could hoping to shove him away from my mother. I was slapped to the ground immediately.

His striking me not only angered my mother, but my brothers and sisters as well. I don't remember how my daddy ended up with the shotgun, but before he knew what was happening, we were all punching and kicking his ass.

He dropped the gun and started hitting my mother in the face. Somehow, while we had been attacking daddy, momma got a hold of the shotgun and began clunking my father over the head with it. Blocking the blows the best he could, he finally got the door open and ran for his life. Momma's nose was trickling blood, and her left eye was swollen shut, but that wasn't shit, she was most definitely the real super woman...

I spent like the first 8 years of my weird and eerie life in that house, and was overwhelmed with relief to have moved out of it...

***

The family moves to a different neighborhood, a complex of Projects in the midst of an affluent community. After a fight at the mostly white school where the Author had faced prejudice and ridicule, he walks...

... on out of the class, on out of the entire building, and headed home.

I made it home about 7:00 p.m. I went straight to the park because I was still debating whether to go home or not. At that time, there were a bunch of problems my family had been submerged in, and the pressure of it all was driving my young ass crazy. I was fed up with not having the materialistic shit I desired, peer pressure had me fighting almost every day at school, and I was sick and tired of being punished by a mother who just didn't understand me.

When I finally decided to go home, it was already time for my mother to be heading out for work. I was well aware of the hellish ass whipping I had coming, so I voted to go ahead and get it over with. As soon as I stepped through the front door, my mother was on her way out for work; work or not, she still had time to get on my ass.

I woke up hours later that night, on the floor of my bed-room; she had done beaten me unconscious with her bare hands.

That same night, I packed my duffle bag full of clothes, and crawled out my window unto a world I knew nothing about...